After the Rainbow: Golden Poems

Zaneta Varnado Johns

Published by Prolific Pulse Press LLC

Library of Congress Control Number: 2022900767

ISBN 978-1-7365620-6-2
ISBN 978-1-7365620-7-9 Gold Signature Edition

Cover Design by: Lisa Tomey, Prolific Pulse Press LLC
Cover Photo: NiShetta's Photography
Interior Photos:
Author & "Reflection" photo, Kyla Cooper & Kyli Cooper: NiShetta's Photography
Lisa Tomey: Lisa Tomey
Ms. Maggie: Maggie Gordon
Cynthia Hightower-Jenkins: Cy Davison
George Bamu: Dr. Paul S. Docktor
Jason Merriweather: Bruce Merriweather
Zan Expressions Logo, Signature Heart Image, and Kyla Cooper reading: Kelli R. Jackson
Pratibha Savani: Pratibha Savani
Sarfraz Ahmed: Sarfraz Ahmed
Darryl Varnado and "We Are They" photos: Author's personal collection
Uncredited photos: Unsplash or license on file: Prolific Pulse Press LLC
prolificpulse@gmail.com
Interior Design by: Lisa Tomey, Prolific Pulse Press LLC

Contents

Dedication vii

Previously Published.. viii

Acknowledgements ix

Foreword... xiii

Gold Plated: Shiny and Flaky, Not Real 1

America's Mold 2

Imagine America...3

01062021USA Shameful 5

How Dare You 7

Gold Filled: Gold Layers Masking Pain 9

Feeling Dissed...10

I'm Just Sayin' 11

Lost Time 12

Quicksand 13

Baggage...14

Not Her Fault 15

To My Dear Friend 17

Our Boulder Valley, in the Shadows of Death................19

What Was Supposed to Be Next? 20

Smoke Signals 22

10K: Officially Gold..23

Who I Am...24

Today 26

Like a Child..27

Spring Morning 28

Compassion in Three Words..29

Perspective 30

North Star..31

Life's Gives and Takes 32

Masks 34

What I Learned from SIP: Sheltering in Place...................35

Rebirth...36

Her Dilemma..37

Anthology 38

Can't Stop, Won't Stop...39

My Last Nerve 40

A Different Kind of Diversity 41

Accountability..43

Garden Notions 44

Poetry in Motion 45

14K: Universal Gold Standard 47

Innocent Joy 48

New Wonderland 49

Caring Exchange 50

Mirror Mirror 52

Bubble Bath...53

Peaceful Slumber 54

Morning Sounds..55

Yearning for Summer 57

Cries from Zan's Closet...58

Kitty Cat Conundrum..60

My Forever Song 61

Casa Magdalena 62

My Favorite Things 63

18K: Refined Golden Sentiments................................65

Born Day Thoughts 2021 66

Empty Space 67

Hand in Hand 68

Steppingstones 69

Abecedarian Wisdom..71

Let's Sing for the Unsung 72

More Alike than Different..74

My Tree...75

Loving Outdoors 76

Joy in My Swing 77

Spinning 78

Stand Taller 79

Look at the Poets 80

22K: Bright Golden Luminaries 81

Colorful Photo...83

Reflection...85

Double Blessings...87

The Man You See 91

She Is..97

Tribute to Amanda Gorman 99

High Voltage: The Love of a Beautiful Lamp 103

Dear Ms. Maggie 107

Tribute to the Africa Agenda 111

Tribute to Jason Merriweather 113

We Are They 115

24K: Pure Solid Gold...................................119

One Day 120

Covered by Prayer..121

No Footprints 122

Everyone Get Ready 123

Whispers from Heaven 125

No More Violence...126

Thanksgiving...127

My Last Prayer..128

About the Author 130

Contributing Poets 132

Gratitude..133

Book Club Dialogue Prompts 135

Golden Nugget...137

What Matters...137

Dedication

"We are surrounded by poetry on all sides."
~Vincent van Gogh~

I am honored to dedicate **After the Rainbow:** *Golden Poems* to the phenomenal giants on whose shoulders I stand. Thank you for setting my steppingstones. My wish is that my walk has made you proud. I remain unrefined yet able to shine because of God's perpetual attention to my impurities. Like myself, my poems begin unrefined. I polish and polish with mindful attention to achieve the golden luster befitting my readers. To every reader who ingests my words, it is my distinct privilege to touch you. I extend a grateful kiss upon your heart as you partake in my expressive drifts of love. Inside you will find truth told, pain revealed, and joy shared. May you be forever blessed knowing that you have blessed me. To the global community of poets, thank you for welcoming me into your circles and garden. My passion for poetry has been fueled by your fervent inspiration. Because of you, I have the audacity to believe that the world must hear my voice.

Previously Published

Also from 2-time bestselling author Zaneta Varnado Johns:

Poetic Forecast*: Reflections on Life's Promises, Storms, and Triumphs*
Voices of the 21ˢᵗ Century*: Resilient Women Who Rise and Make a Difference* (Co-author)

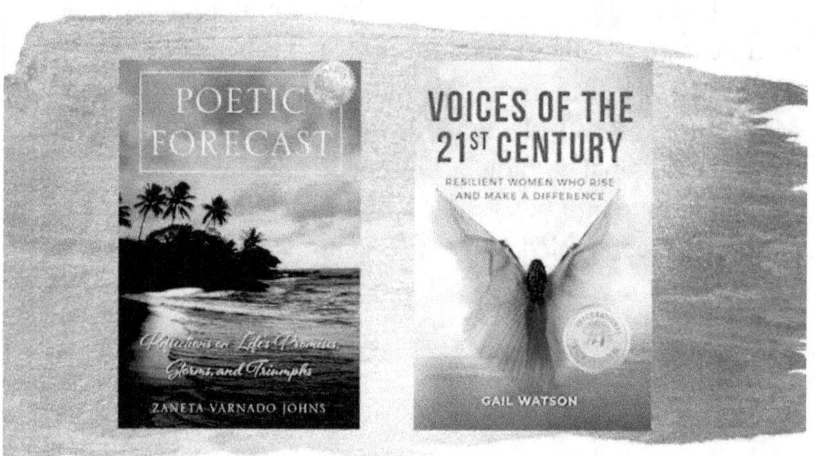

Acknowledgements

I am honored to have poems judged and selected as worthy of inclusion in these distinguished literary works. Some features may reflect earlier versions. Thank you to all of the dedicated editors who introduce our work to the world.

Fine Lines Literary Journal, Autumn 2021~ "Tribute to Amanda Gorman"
Open Door Magazine, September 2021~ "We Are They"
Open Door Magazine, October 2021~ Author Feature including poems: "We Are They," "Mirror, Mirror," "Reflection," "What Matters"
Open Door Magazine Anthology,~ "We Are They"
Around the World: Cityscapes and Landscapes, November 2021~ "We Are They"
Songs of Peace Anthology, December 2021~ "No More Violence"
A Safe & Brave Space Anthology of Poetry and Art, November 2021~ "Joy in My Swing," "Garden Notions," "Covered by Prayer"
Jane Austen, an anthology of thoughts & opinions, June 2021~ "More Alike than Different"
Animal Friends: a WAM writers collective VIII, December 2021~ "Kitty Cat Conundrum"
Open Door Magazine, December 2021~ "Peaceful Slumber"
Real Women Write, Volume 20, Beyond COVID:
Leaning into Tomorrow anthology, December 2021~ "What I Learned from SIP: Sheltering in Place," "Abecedarian Wisdom"
The Literary Parrot-Series Two, December 2021~ "A Different Kind of Diversity"
PLCS Women's Issues Anthology, "Not Her Fault," "No Footprints"

Stories & Poems in the Song of Life anthology, February 2022~ "My Forever Song"
Voices of the 21st Century: Conscious Caring Women Who Make a Difference (Co-Author), February 2022~ "Caring Exchange," "Mirror Mirror"
Passion of Poetry Anthology, February 2022~ "Colorful Photo," "One Day," "New Wonderland"

Read More:

Additional creative expressions by Poet Zaneta Varnado Johns are featured in the following publications:

Fine Lines Literary Journal, Summer 2021, "After the Reset"
A Love Letter (or Poem) To . . ., December 2021, "Dear Oprah"
Fine Lines Literary Journal, Winter 2021, "A Mother's Intuition"
Jack Tomlinson Anthology, TBD—Late 2022, "Let's Sing for the Unsung"
Social Justice Inks, TBD-2022, "Blood Rights," (with Sarfraz Ahmed), "Now You Know," "Thinking Out Loud," "Brown Bear," "Simple Creed," and "What Does the Mirror Say?"

*We the people were
designed to love*

*It is our faultless
virtue and purpose*

When the sun returns after the rain
I search for rainbows…
I am *Joy*. I am *Peace*. I am *Happy*!
From "Loving Outdoors"
Zaneta Varnado Johns

Foreword
James J. Johns II

Into each life, storms are bound to come. But right when it seems the darkest, the storm breaks, the sun shines through and a rainbow appears giving hope and peace where a few minutes prior there was turmoil and grief.

You hold a golden treasure in your hands! Over the past year I have had the pleasure of witnessing poet Zaneta "Zan" Varnado Johns emerge from life's challenges and opportunities with a strength and wisdom that reflects the character of her soul. She mined the soil of her soul and discovered gold! This inspired her to pen her most recent book entitled **After the Rainbow**, which succeeds her #1 bestselling debut book of poetry **Poetic Forecast**, published in 2020.

After the Rainbow poses questions which are intended to provoke thought without judgement. Zan's style is conversational and rhythmic, and while her message is clear, her prose is unique, sometimes rhyming, sometimes not. As you embark on this journey with the author, prepare to enjoy poignant poems about social justice, sorrow, hope, and joy. Zan goes deep within her soul to process the ills of our society and yet emerges hopeful.

In the past year, Zan has been blessed with the opportunity to collaborate with poets from around the world. Three featured poems were co-authored with esteemed poets Sarfraz Ahmed and Pratibha Savani from the United Kingdom. Additionally, her poems are featured on the dedication page in the 2021 and 2022 international bestselling series, **Voices of the 21st Century**.

Zan has the divine ability to celebrate people. In addition to celebrating loved ones, she has a gift for capturing the essence of those she has never personally met with the same clarity and beauty usually reserved for people one has long histories with. **After the Rainbow** features a poem commissioned by a father whose son unexpectedly passed away; a poem celebrating Amanda Gorman's ground-shattering recitation at President Joe Biden's inauguration; a poem paying tribute after the passing of a beautiful celebrity whom Johns met on social media; and a poem celebrating a family friend's ninety-first birthday. These poems are found in the chapter entitled, "22K: Bright Golden Luminaries."

From the first chapter, "Gold Filled," to the final chapter, "24K: Pure Solid Gold," Zan offers hope for a brighter tomorrow. You, the lucky reader, have struck gold!

Refined by the Fire of God
James J. Johns II

The Word says count it all joy when you meet trials
of various kinds
To endure more pain in this life, are you out of your mind?
To rejoice in trials seems so insane,
Why would mankind want to endure *more* pain?
But our trials are like the heat used to purify gold
That refining process is ages old.
The temperature of the heat is designed to ensure
that impurities get removed, so the gold can be made pure.
Like gold ore, it's the impurities that cloud our souls
So, God turns up the heat so we can be made whole.
Too much heat would cause pain and despair
But God said he wouldn't give us more than we can bear
So, count it all joy and not a loss
When God turns up the heat to expose the dross.
When the refining process is finally through
You will see God's reflection looking back at you.
In this book of poems, my wife Zan endeavors to share
Some of life's trials that made her aware,
That the trials in our lives are not considered strife
But through them, God reveals to us the true meaning of life.
So, as you read her passages, try not to overlook
That it's the trials we've endured
that helped her write this book.
She reminds us all that while on Earth we trod
Like gold, we're being refined by the fire of God.

God said he wouldn't give us more than we can bear
So, count it all joy and not a loss
When God turns up the heat to expose the dross.

Gold Plated: Shiny and Flaky, Not Real

America's Mold

For far too long, we have boasted
of America's mold
as crafted by the founders.
This country's perfect mold
whose constitutional goal
was a more perfect union.
This imperfect mold that
robbed America's true natives—
its rightful founders…without apology
This broken deceitful mold
that cries loudly today.

America wails because of
its other mold—its fungus
toxic and airborne
prolific and turbulent
Its lies…its injustice
its greed that bred fear
its fear that bred hatred
its hatred which spread
at the rate of fungus
This lethal mold is buried in the
foundation of America's mold.

Be not discouraged because love won
Love and empathy can cleanse
the spores of hatred,
lowering its concentrations
We the people were designed to love
It is our faultless virtue and purpose
Let us love on purpose
Let us eradicate
America's shameful mold.

Imagine America

Imagine our world if Eve never bit the apple.
Then imagine America if we could
      un-sail Columbus' ship!
      un-steal native land!
      un-massacre Native Americans!

Reality check—Columbus arrived.
Now, imagine America if we could
      un-capture future slaves
      untie hanging nooses
      un-ignite flaming crosses
      un-whip bended backs
      un-sever fugitives' limbs

Imagine the America as written by our founders.
If only we could
      un-diminish women
      un-ignore the poor
      un-drop the atomic bomb
      un-intern Japanese Americans
      un-fear African Americans
      un-deport Mexican Americans
      un-harass Asian Americans

Imagine America's safety
if we could
      un-punch the abused
      un-rape the unguarded
      un-medicate the vulnerable
      un-pull too many triggers
      uninvent the gun
      un-kneel that policeman's knee!

Imagine America
If we could simply not discriminate!
If we could un-wrong the wrongs
and make everything right!
Imagine!

01062021USA Shameful

I was joyfully admiring pearls
loving the anticipation
of women
strong women
beautiful women
surviving women
elderly women
baby girls
young girls
all adorned in pearls
eager to celebrate
our first Madam Vice President
Kamala Harris
on January 20th!

Why did I turn on the news!
I went from pearls to hatred
Anguish—unleashed, un-policed
unwelcomed yet welcomed
publicly *loved,*
cheered and incited
by the sitting president
of the United States of America!

They stormed our capitol
with rampant disregard
for what is right—
attempting to steal
the will of
the American people
They killed, they injured
They bragged and boasted
It was shameful!

Our democracy
could've been shattered
but I know
God is watching
I know it had to happen
We had to witness
bold hate in action
to intentionally pursue
the victory of love
Love—my word for 2021
I remain hopeful
I remain watchful
Let's not panic.
Let's not give up.
Be still and know…
LOVE wins!

How Dare You

That Black Man—once a child
His mother's answered prayer
The apple of his father's eye
My brother, *my* husband, *my* son
God's gift to this world
How dare you want to hurt him!
Why do you
          dishonor his greatness
          reject his prestige
          dismiss his rights
How dare you!

That Black woman—who nursed this nation
fed your children
Unwittingly birthed *your* children
She is our queen, the nucleus of her family
She is virtuous in God's eyes
How dare you diminish *my* contribution!
Why would you
          deny *my* peace
          resent *my* strength
          disrespect *me*
How dare you!

That Black boy and Black girl—
My children, *my* grandchildren
are precious in His sight
as precious as every child
deserving of every privilege
afforded to *your* child.
How dare you deny their rights!

How could you
        not protect them
        not value their lives
        not fulfill their dreams
How dare you!
And that Black family, like *your* family
is deep-rooted in this nation
which does all it can to dismantle it
How dare you not seek justice or equality
        for this family, *my* family
America, how dare you!

Gold Filled: Gold Layers Masking Pain

Feeling Dissed

TV's breaking news gives me the blues
I wonder, and I pray,
does anyone else feel this way?

Disrespected, disgruntled, disgusted, dismissed, disowned,
Discredited, disconcerted, disrupted, dismayed, dissatisfied,
Disappointed, disillusioned, disliked, disgraced, disinherited,
Disarmed, disbanded, or discombobulated!

I become distracted and disinterested.
Displeased, I disengage and distance myself.
I boldly disconnect the TV and disappear!

I'm Just Sayin'

Please, don't take my kindness for weakness
or my humility for meekness.
I am a force to be reckoned with.
When mistreated, my response is swift.
You had better see me as God sees me,
as majestic as a redwood tree!

I am fierce, I am able—I can do anything.
Whatever I pray, my God will bring.
I slumber with ease
knowing God is pleased.
I wake up knowing that today will be great—
because I am in it!
I am here
I am light
I am love . . .
Just sayin'!

Lost Time

How many tick-tocks must we forfeit?
Time taken for granted is lost.
With no promise of tomorrow,
prolonged silence has its cost.

If tomorrow is not to be,
how would you spend today?
Would you long to be near me?
Or do you favor staying away?

Do you miss the zealous desire?
Do you yearn for reconnection?
Have you forgotten the excitement
when you'd head in my direction?

Just think of those beautiful drives
toward the valley and foothills.
You knew I'd be breathlessly waiting
with open arms, wine properly chilled.

We were younger and ever so elated
to be together once again.
A movie, bike ride, concert, or dinner—
together is what mattered then.

Together matters now!

Quicksand

Loose murky grains of sand
provoked, agitated, lush with pain
It's a frightening point of no return,
dark and consuming.

The sand is quick—
can't hold our weight.
I refuse to be sucked in.

To become light,
we must shed what no longer serves us.
To avoid perish,
we must open our minds and hearts.
Hands up…
Let's breathe!

Baggage

When an emotional cart overflows
with all-consuming baggage,
moving forward is crushing.

A packed cart sharply accelerates
downhill at full throttle.

Aggressive winds of change
cast a shadow of darkness
on an altered spirit
devoid of cheer.

Anger appears in a face too familiar—
no smile, no laughter, no light.

Sudden withdrawal is
a costly calamity.
A demeanor beset by baggage
is chilling.

Heavy toxic baggage,
not worthy of recycling—
       impenetrable
       impermeable
       impervious

Empty the cart…

Purge the numbing torment…

Eliminate the baggage before it becomes
impossible to reconcile!

Not Her Fault

She left for the party looking like a million bucks.
She returned home like a discarded penny—
Her appearance was amuck.
Her elation swelled when they first drove away.
She had lustful hopes after a long stressful day.
They laughed, they danced, they ate and drank.
When a handsome man winked at her,
to him and his ego, it felt like a prank.

Her once cheerful companion did a one-eighty turn.
His demeanor was all anger—a fiery rage that could burn.
He grabbed his beautiful queen and reduced her to fear.
Like a ragdoll, she went limp as her eyes filled with tears.
He said things to her not worthy of repeat.
His words were as harsh as a drumline's rapid beat.
Her lovely dress was torn, her arm needed a sling.
Every time she wiped her eyes,
the fresh abrasions would sting.

She wondered what she'd done to cause such a scene.
She assumed it was her fault,
though like grass in summer, his envy was green.
She softly said, "I'm sorry," holding onto her purse.
He furiously snatched her by the arm,
making the painful strain worse.
Her strand of pearls was now broken,
but not as much as her heart.
She'd ignored all the signs
that he revealed from the start.

They drove home in silence—
he never spoke a word.
She thought about their last dance
and the awful things she'd heard.

She slowly stumbled inside, ran a bath, and got some ice.
He brewed a cup of tea to sweetly serve her,
pretending to be nice.
She sat in utter silence—her lips could not move.
There was nothing he could do,
and her deep pains…he could not soothe.
She knew it was time to leave her toxic man.
She fervently prayed throughout the night,
She awakened determined and said, "I CAN!"

To My Dear Friend

I treasure the lifelong memories we share
You already know how much I care
The battle you face is a giant, I know
Your testimony will help others grow

May you have peace knowing you are loved
May you be comforted by angels above
I love you dearly—I always have
Our friendship adds a hopeful salve

I admire your strength and faithful will
God knows your prayers and will fulfill
Your heart's desires are in His hands
Your comfort and healing are in His plans

I pray for your wellness through and through
I pray for your lovely granddaughter too
I know your guardians smile from above
As we shower you with endless love

You've always had a heart of gold
Your charity lives in stories untold
I love the way you give to others
You reflect the goodness of your mother

You helped the youth and gave advice
Tough love you shared while being nice
Your voice radiates spiritual sounds
Your humor delights everyone around

When you share stories as only you can
My heartfelt laughter spurs tears to land
I await the day when you have no pain
I trust your strength you'll soon regain.

Our Boulder Valley, in the Shadows of Death

Boulder, Colorado was never innocent.
Its history, like most, not without blemishes
of injustice or pain…
Yet it boasts of progression,
acknowledges its past and attempts to
right its wrongs.

Our beautiful valley with its splendid flatirons,
its notorious Hill, its award-winning
University of Colorado
is now forever marred
by these shadows of senseless deaths!
Innocent lives lost—too many, too soon
on this third day of Spring in Boulder, Colorado.
Thank God for the heroes on this painfully sad day.

Boulder didn't deserve to be
tarnished by domestic terror.
Nor do all the other cities around the world.
It didn't deserve this tragedy
on lovely Table Mesa Drive,
at the base of NCAR—
the heart of SoBo.
It doesn't deserve that heart-wrenching
pinpoint on America's map of domestic tragedies.

No city does!

What Was Supposed to Be Next?
Remembering Boulder, Colorado's King Soopers Tragedy

Abandoned shopping carts in disarray
A horrific image of mankind gone astray!
Grocery shopping brutally interrupted
I wonder what supposed to be next…

What was for dinner, now cancelled forever!
When you shuffled through the snow,
did you sanitize carts once more?
Were you shopping for the week,
Was your cart filled to peak?
Who did you encounter on your way in?
I hope you were greeted with a neighborly grin.
Was your shopping list in your phone
or secured in your mind?
Was a crumpled list left on the floor
for others to later find?

Were you planning to buy flowers
to brighten someone else's day?
Did you grab a treat near the magazine display?
Perhaps you bought Tylenol, tissue, soup, or juice
Was there a loved one at home waiting
patiently for fruit?

Did you stop by the deli to select fish or meat
Were you there for broccoli, peppers, or beets?
Was your lettuce Romaine to couple with tomatoes
Did you pick up asparagus or choose sweet potatoes?
I believe God wept as you ran for your life.
You did nothing to deserve that dreadful strife!

I pray for your loved ones left here to mourn
I pray that time eases this tragedy's thorns.
May your disrupted life not be in vain.
May our safe surroundings soon be reclaimed.

Smoke Signals

What is the message in the smoke
that eerily floats across our landscape
of purple mountains majesty?

Smoke signals, dense and vast—
a slow and hovering shower of ash.
Was it sent to mask the darkness
in this troubled world of ours?
Or maybe to cover sins,
declaring God's almighty power?

Perhaps it came to visually exclaim
what we refused to hear.
Remember God's whispers in the
floods and tornadoes,
followed by the earth's quakes and shouts?
We ignored the roar of hurricane after hurricane
but can't ignore the pandemic or droughts!

Through the raging smoke, God's voice
screams at our eyes and noses.
His signals inflame our smoke-filled lungs.
Can you feel and hear the proclamation?
Daughters and sons, take heed.
Give Mother Earth what she needs.
Please, listen to the smoke!

10K: Officially Gold

Who I Am

Girl born on Thursday
If I were born in Africa,
my name might be Yawa or Aba or Yaba.
Born instead in New Orleans—
the Crescent City—
I am Zaneta, named by my mother.
It means "God is gracious"
It is the blueprint for my life!

A baby boomer, my mother's "baby girl"
Preceded by four siblings,
followed by one: my baby brother—
born one year later, plus a day.
September babies, Virgos.
Like my Chinese zodiac sign—
the rooster—I am
warm-hearted, bright, and honest.

It was 1957 when I arrived
on that fifth day of September.
The Little Rock Crisis
erupted eighteen days later.
Six weeks later,
Elvis rocked the jailhouse.
I'd like to think that my arrival
rocked the world…
if only in the ego of my mind.

I am the light of God's amazing grace.
I humbly celebrate all that I am
and all that I am yet to become.
A mother, grandmother,
wife, sister, aunt, and friend
I am a resilient woman
I am a conscious caring woman
I make a difference…I rock!
God is gracious indeed!

Today

Today is yesterday's promise—
Fulfilled.

Celebrate!
Help someone!
Make a difference!

Remember that yesterday
you could only imagine
tomorrow's promise.

It's here…
Don't waste it!

Like a Child
By Sarfraz Ahmed and Zaneta Varnado Johns

My stomach churns,
Twists and turns,
Acid burns,
As I wait,
For the sound of your keys,
At the door,

Like a child learning to crawl,
I try and stand up,
But I can't help falling down,
I want to scream and shout,
But I can't get the words out,

My whole world twists and turns,
Upside down, in and out,
From the four corners of my mouth,

My smile becomes a frown.
A crushed tattoo pointing down,
As I sit to steady the pit,
Held deep within my soul.

When I hear the key,
I want to leap toward you with glee.
I love you more than I love the earth.
Embrace me like a child.
Only then can I feel my worth.

Spring Morning

Today awaits your awakening
Leave your restful slumber
Your friend, the dove, sings hello
He declares what looms outside—
splendor, infinite possibilities
Your daily choice of nature's delights
is ready to be served.

The snow is gone
Long-awaited new buds adorn the trees
      tulips peek
      bunnies hop
      birds nest…

Spring has sprung with hope and promise
Excitedly, you open the blinds
You smile, feeling blessed
Slowly, you wrap the blind's cord
around its place holder—
set there by magnificent hands.

You inhale the smell of freshly brewed coffee
poured moments earlier by those same
magnificent hands.
You anticipate what's to come,
gleefully expecting far more.
Springtime is here
It is a good morning for real.

Compassion in Three Words

Say a prayer
Shed a tear
Lift a hand
Open a door
Send a note
Make a call
Lend a hand
Share a meal
Hug a child
Visit an elder
Rub a back
Keep a secret
Wipe a tear
Write a note
Lend an ear
Hold a hand
Stand for something!

Perspective

On the forms we completed in grade school,
I innocently checked "middle-class"
for my family's income status.
No one told me we were middle-class,
but I knew we were not rich.
In my naïve elementary mind,
we were not poor either.

I had everything I needed.
    Two loving hardworking parents
    Two doting Godparents
    Two to a bed
    Two hot meals and lunch
    At least, two good friends!

When answering a multiple-choice question,
the last unselected option is the correct answer,
correct?

Middle-class I chose with a middle-class mindset
in the middle of Louisiana's segregated
lower-than-middle class neighborhoods.

Rich in love—upper-class where it mattered.
Mindset is everything!

North Star

Omnipresent landmark
        absolute and true
bright and clear
steady and stationary
compass of inspiration
Celestial anchor
Unwavering
Dependable
Purposeful
Constant
Guiding
Gift

I am beyond humbled
I am truly honored
to be called a north star!

Life's Gives and Takes

Give a little. Take a lot.
Give up. Never give up.
Give in. Never give in.

Take it easy. Give me a break.
Take note. Take heed.
Take your time. Take over.

Give a minute. Take a minute.
Give away. Take away.

Take it back. Give it back.
Take a day. Give a talk.
Take a break. Take a walk.
Take up space. Give me room.
Take my breath away.

Give and receive.
Give your all. Take it all in.
Give an organ. Give hope.
Give life. Take a nap.

Take a leave. Give it a rest.

Give a care. Give a damn.

Take your temp. Give it time.
Take your turn. Give your best.
Take it all. Take his name.
Take out the trash.

Give a hug. Give a hand.

Take a chance. Give it a shot.
Take his nerve. Take a hike.

Give a hint. Take for granted.

Take nothing for granted.
Take a shot. Take over.
Take good care!

Masks

I wear this mask for you and me.
As we gingerly approach each other,
I feel safer seeing your mask…
I wonder, can you see the smile in my eyes—my smize?
Can you feel my silent prayer for you and us?
I care about you
I respect your space
I smile because I'm glad to see you
wearing that mask!

For those without the mask,
your choice is troubling…
yet it is yours.
I respect your liberty to choose.
Though I wonder, do you wish me well?
Don't worry because I'm all prayed up.
I cannot smile but I pray for you and us.
Moreover, I wish you well!

What I Learned from SIP: Sheltering in Place

Half full, half empty: either way,
you're the other half of my cup.
God's timing is incredibly punctual.
I crave social interaction, but I covet stillness.
Quietness is loud and very much appreciated.
Ample space is a generous gift.
I won't be well until you're well.
A child's infinite wonder makes the worst things bearable.
Everyone has a pearl of wisdom to offer.
If you haven't found joy, try looking inside.
Simple things are being discovered; thank you SIP!
Be intentional; connection comes in various forms.
I like beautiful things, but I don't need all of them.
If you're troubled by painful thoughts, remove the thorn.
Life's storms bring rain. When the sun returns,
seek out the rainbows.
Wake up expecting to make a difference.
Imagine the impending smile of someone you plan to help.
Don't ignore your talents; when you're ready for them,
they might be gone.
Passion is everything they said it is.
Kind words are soothing; hug someone with your words.
Let's make "love" our next pandemic!

Rebirth

To be rebirthed again is to have another shot
To start anew, fresh, free, protected…

To abandon the torment that
triggered your inner retreat…

To distance yourself from darkness
as you bravely follow the light…

To trust your thoughts and trust yourself
to take care of yourself…

To treasure every second—to greet
possibilities and blossom…

To be rebirthed again is to emerge
justifiably esteemed—
victorious—
      ready to shed despair
      ready to sing
      ready to love yourself.

Her Dilemma

She tenderly leaned into him
naturally blushing, she posed
for that snapshot—
affectionately close
proud and possessive
simply gorgeous
utterly content.

I'm sure eyes rolled
at every attentive table
I just cannot imagine
how many people loved her
while lusting for her man…

And though he loved her
he loved that too!

Anthology

I love anthologies—poetry or prose
Always happy to read one of those.
Proud to be featured as a writer myself
Another publication for my own bookshelf.

Our voices speak volumes
creative expressions from distinct lives
in a bound literary gallery of exclusive canvases.
Canvases painted by multicolored hands
holding multicolored pens.

Every expression's presence on the canvas
bears common or widespread messages—
messages created by diverse trains of thought—
thoughts penned by diverse souls—
souls from diverse places—
places of interest from around the world.

Our submissions convey scholarly prowess
with intentional vulnerability.
We have a hopeful expectation of acceptance.
Thoughtfully judged and selected,
some are chosen as worthy
of inclusion with the others…
to be forever featured as one
in the coveted anthology of poetry or prose!

Can't Stop, Won't Stop

Redefined, repurposed, recharged
Repositioned for the rest of my life
There is no turning back
I applaud the past
I embrace the now
I pivot and leap toward the future
I use what I did to do what I do
I use what I got to get what I want
I passionately pursue my purpose
I am growing and glowing…
Ain't no stopping me now!

My Last Nerve

Your shenanigans nearly took my nerve.
You've got me feeling quite perturbed.
When I look up, you say look down.
Whenever I smile, you cast a frown.

When I tell you that the sky is blue,
you defiantly say it isn't true.
I gave you almost everything I had
when all you did was made me sad.

I'm exhausted—can't take anymore.
Grab your things and dot the door!
This nerve is all that I have left
I vow to keep it for myself!

I'm serious Dear, you've got to go.
I've had it with you from head to toe!
Walk straight ahead, avoid the curves.
Take everything except my last nerve!

A Different Kind of Diversity

One student tentatively walked alone to school
Another had little sleep—awakened by nightmares
One hurts from sleeping in the cold outdoors
Another has not eaten since yesterday's free lunch
One was touched all night in all the wrong places
Another hides bruises for fear of scolding
One child is ashamed of his family's heritage
Next to him a girl hides her ethnic lunch
In the corner sits a boy who feels like a girl
Staring at a girl who feels like a boy
One child feels worthless as repeatedly told
Another won't speak because of her accent
One child grieves his beloved pet
Another lost a sibling during a traffic stop
One child is hoping to soon be adopted
Another is surrounded by endless love
One witnessed her parents taken away in handcuffs
Another worries about his mother's black eye
One child limps and dreads ridicule
Another is bullied but afraid to report
One is fretful because her friends ignore her
Another hides and listens for gunshots
One was promoted although he cannot read
Another is autistic, trapped in her own mind
One was told that he is better than others
Others were taught that we all have value
Many are prepared and ready to learn
Some are not equipped yet eager to learn

All children are worthy of equal investment
their minds wide open
their hearts full of love
Every child deserves a safe bright future
Every child is our future's best shot at peace
The right teacher entrusted with this
classroom of children
will greet them with compassion
will meet them at their needs
will empower them with knowledge
will encourage them to read
An empowered empathetic teacher
can break the cycle of hatred and fear.

Accountability

Someone asked,
How many words have I typed?
How many poems have I written?
How much paper have I used?
How much ink have I printed?
How many hours do I write?

A better question is:
How much love have I shared?
Ask me that and nothing else!

Garden Notions

Grow your vision inside the Garden
All flowers are welcome, thorns included
Reach for a hand, flourish together
Dare to love out loud…on paper
Enter as you are…leave better
No pressure or judgement blooms here.

Opportunities exist for cross-creative germination
Find your circle…blossom where you're planted.

Nurture your intuition and muse
Engage with others—poets need other poets
Utilize all corners of this creative haven
Respect the serenity of this safe and brave space
Our inspirational calling is our sacred bond.

Poetry in Motion

Like wheels turning in motion,
my ink glides across the page
Gripping the paper with traction
rolling smoothly with the flow
of my mind
I write intentionally and steady
My thoughts gear up to rise up
My twists and turns lead
to everywhere
I stop only to help someone else
along my journey
I keep my eyes on the road—
my page
Mirrors assist—all angles.
I tell the mirror what to say
It remembers my words and
sings back to me
Poetry in motion—
Every word transports love
to varied destinations
Some words travel slowly
Some words are swift
like a race car—fast.
Regardless, they touch, love and last.

THIS SPACE IS NOT EMPTY · · LOVE LIVES HERE · ·

14K: Universal Gold Standard

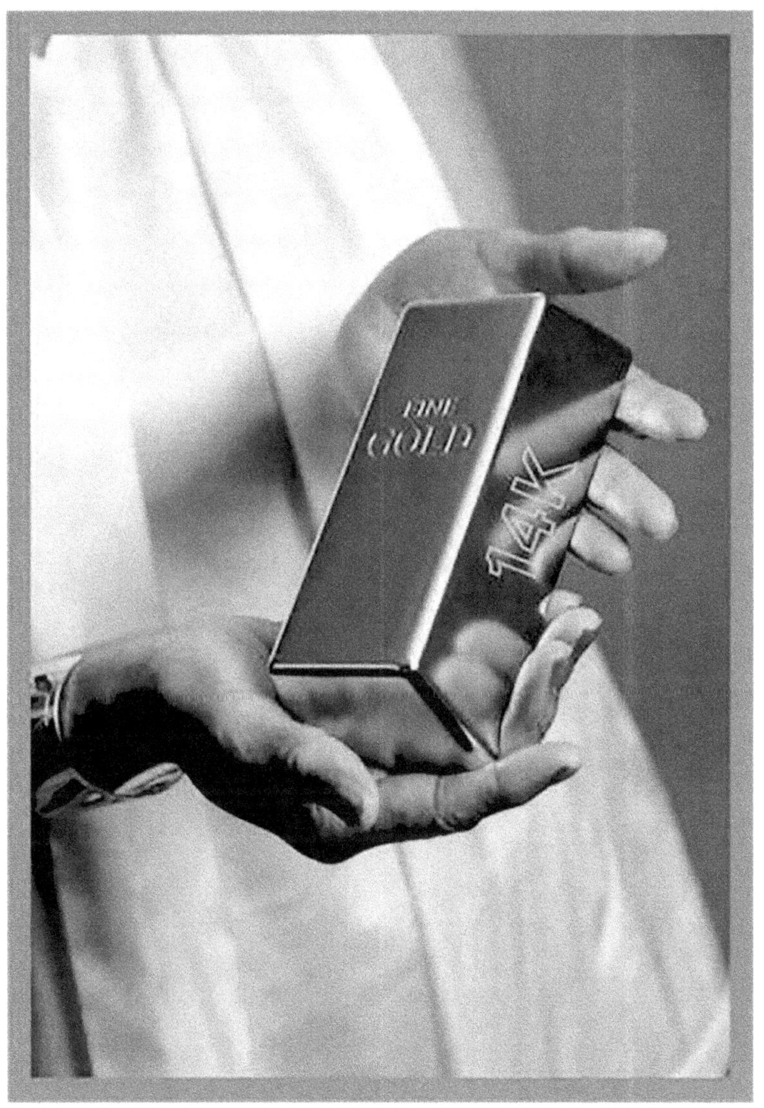

Innocent Joy

It's all joy beneath the umbrellas
Summer blankets on the grass—none alike
Five or six little girls—alike and different
unaware of the world's obsession with sameness

Huddled in bliss on their perfect outdoor carpets
consumed by friendship and wonder
as their brothers chase footballs and flags

They trade stories and snacks
laughter and smiles
innocent joy and love—what matters…

They revel in the shade without expectation
oblivious to all that is brewing
outside their cozy space beneath the umbrellas.

New Wonderland
By Zaneta Varnado Johns and Pratibha Savani

On this rock I contemplate
the water's voice below
Trees shelter me from what's beyond
and frame the river's flow

I accept nature's invitation
to travel the path of faith
Our Savior walked and left a trail
to save the human race

Standing at the edge of life
I see a boat from afar, leaving
Following that enormous trail
Bringing me one step closer to believing

And the clouds above me shield the sun
But its infinite light remains
I'm guided by the knowledge that
my life is not in vain

With my faith in hand
Humanity living on a strand
I'm setting off into that majestic boat
For a much better tomorrow, in new wonderland

Caring Exchange

You enter a park lined with benches—
on each sits a woman who cares.
Imagine their hands extended toward you,
and their minds of subconscious prayers.

Imagine their hopes, imagine their dreams.
Conscious women are living full lives.
They are doctors, teachers, executives, and such,
business owners, writers, and wives.

One says, smiling, "Come, sit or stand.
I have lessons and stories to tell."
You sit by her and smile when she adds,
"Welcome, your presence is swell!"

She leans in and asks what is on your mind.
Her compassion is touching your soul.
You also have stories and lessons to share—
and some secrets you have never told.

She says, "Take your time, dear Sister.
Please relax, I offer my time to you.
Share your secrets—share your stories.
The world needs to hear your truth."

You ponder her request to open your heart,
then you proceed to inquire about hers.
Both invitations are genuine because
a mutual exchange is preferred.

Together you trade stories of joy and pain
as you laugh and you cry out loud.
You stand taller when finished—your load is lighter.
You are emotionally and spiritually endowed!

Mirror Mirror

Mirror Mirror, speak to me.
What exactly do you see?
Am I enough—
Need I change?
Should anything be rearranged?
I will make a difference in the world
as I encourage other girls.
Will there be others who encourage me
to be the best that I can be?
My children will see their mother's strength
and laud their own without pretense.
How many hurdles threaten my path?
When I meet trouble, will it last?
Worthy feats are what I crave.
I need role models who are brave.
Send me wisdom.
Send me grace.
Empower me throughout my lifelong race!

Bubble Bath

Don't question my loyalty
but you should envy
my bubble bath—
my faithful lover
who waits for me
every night.
He is always hot
always wet
no questions asked…
smells good too!
He knows what I need—
knows what I like.
When I move,
he moves
We splash, we dance,
we connect.
At the end,
he is drained.
His passionate task
is finished.
Our affair is over…
until tomorrow!

Peaceful Slumber

I pray…I lie down…I snuggle
I close my eyes and submit.
While I sleep, safely and comfortably,
the world turns.

I rest all night, a sacred gift,
not taken for granted.
Trusting that all is well—
for eight hours—nightly I dream

Uninterrupted
Unencumbered
Unbothered
No rushing
No seeking
No worrying
No regrets!

Peaceful slumber, one of my most
coveted blessings in life!

Morning Sounds

Oh, how I prefer
the sweet sounds of morning
Not the rude alarm jolting me
out of my cozy slumber—
determined to do exactly what
I asked it to do last night.
I half-heartedly await its dreadful
sound—startled nonetheless!

Annoyed by the flushing toilet
I roll my still sleepy eyes!
My angry ears cringe at the sound
of water rushing and swishing…
so rowdy it makes me want to pee!
Then comes the sink's loud waterfall
formed by hot and cold levers
left unattended—running at max!
Envision the sound of another's teeth
being fervently brushed…
a throat, meekly gargled
spit, forcefully spat
the sink, dutifully rinsed.

Slowly I rise, silently giving thanks
I greet the day with a grateful smile,
sipping tea as I listen for the sweet,
preferred sounds of morn.
I adore the bird's soft song
I love the gentle wind announcing a change
I delight in the humming of
a neighbor's mower

A random siren piques my interest
The coyote's wail follows the dog's bark
I love the far away sound of a plane
or helicopter or an occasional train
Some days, I hear rain.

When the caffeine kicks in,
I welcome the sound of music.
I await his "good morning" whisper
I am alive and thankful that I can hear!

Yearning for Summer

By Zaneta Varnado Johns and Sarfraz Ahmed

In my swing beneath the tree of palms,
I've got summer on my mind.
I yearn for the chance to swim or dance.
As we take two steps toward the beach,
Our scantily clad bodies gleefully waltz.
Walk hand in hand,
As we two-step in the sand.
Let the foaming waves tickle our toes,
As we allow the rush of pristine waters to calm our souls.

We could lose ourselves here for days,
Lying underneath the sun's golden rays,
To luxuriate,
Let the sun glisten and radiate,
I want to dive right in,
Let the water soothe my skin,
Let the foaming waves tickle our toes,
As we allow the rush of pristine waters to calm our souls.

Cries from Zan's Closet

"Remember me," exclaimed the wedding dress.
"I'm elegant. I'm simple.
I'm simply hoping to be worn again.
I still fit but Girl,
you're not getting married again!
Make another bride happy.
Gift the joy you felt as I adorned your body
all those years ago."

"Umph, I'm St. John, and I'm still waiting
to get off this hanger.
You were proud to bring me home.
I like it here, but I want to go somewhere nice!
I am anxiously waiting—hangin'
with my siblings, the other St. Johns.
We are timeless, I know,
but it's getting hot and crowded in here!"

"Hush, please don't all talk at once,"
someone exclaimed.
"One at a time, okay, next…"

"Umm, how many leather jackets
does one woman need!
Didn't you give some away,
and sell some, and consign some?
The problem is you keep buying some!
Girl, stop, just stop!
There's way too many of us
huddled together in this closet!"

"Well, if the leathers can complain
may we speak," uttered the furs.

"Are you that cold or just obsessed?
Either way, you can only wear us one by one.
Girl don't even think about buying another coat!
By the way, please donate some of
those jean jackets too!"

"Hmm, did I hear something,"
she thought.
"Yes, you did!
Honey, don't you know that
boots are made for walkin'!
You have way too many boots
and far too many shoes."
So bored, they started stompin'
while talkin' to each other…
Then the purses shouted, "Hush puppies!"

Speakin' of purses,
like rabbits, they seem to multiply.
Purse-in, purse-in,
not much purse-out goin' on!
At this rate, the purses rule!
That is, provided the jewelry remains silent.
Pray for silence because the jewelry could
start a closet riot and win!

Let's just say, Girl, you got style.
Hopefully, you have places to go
and time—because wearing all this stuff
is gon' take you awhile!

Kitty Cat Conundrum

Work crisis interrupted, I answered my phone,
"Zan Varnado, may I help you," then I heard his tone.
With elation he phoned to proudly say,
"I got a new cat, a black one, today!"
I envisioned that twinkle abound in his eyes;
those glistening sparkles kept me mesmerized.
A year or so ago,
how was I to know
that he loved cats and I did not.
His happy news put me on the spot!
Would my new Boo accept and understand
that his beloved new pet didn't fit my plan…
Cats caused my son's eyelids to fully close;
gave him an uncomfortably itchy nose.
I believed that black cats sparked bad luck;
their motives and movements, I did not trust!
"Noodles" was his new love, what could I do—
two sassy women vying for only one Boo.
Our toothbrushes lived thirty miles apart,
but if "Noodles" won, it would break my heart!
Later, eye drops, then Afrin appeared everywhere.
My Boo was always stuffy, his eyes in despair.
Despite that fact, "Noodles" had the upper hand
shacking up daily, in company with my man!
But my Boo couldn't breathe, he constantly sneezed.
"Your cat is the problem," said the allergist with ease.
A new home for "Noodles" was reluctantly found
and now thirty years later, I wear the crown…
Our toothbrushes reside at the same address…
My Boo breathes freely without airway distress!

My Forever Song

You are my song—unforgettable
         softly crooned
         music optional
precious intimate memories
coveted, cherished, and pure.

Indwell my heart,
my forever love
Speak to me in song
Stop me in my tracks
with your alluring lyrics
         proud
         tender
         soothing
         perfect
Softly serenade my heart forever.

Casa Magdalena

Su casa es mi casa!
Short-term stay, long-term impact.
Your adobe dwelling claimed a piece of my soul.
Or was it the other way around?
Your seductive welcome tells me
that love lives here.
Each careful detail says so.
Your charming flair and great taste lend
a warm sense of home to all who enter.

I unwind in a vintage rocker, beside a small table—
eight angles, sized just right.
How many sat here before me, I wonder.
Did they rock or were they still?
Did they read or listen to music?
I do both.

I face a bed of comfort—a murphy bed perhaps,
covered in southwestern love—an Aztec bronze
layer adorned with turquoise, my favorite.
Antique dressers await my things.

The angular fireplace sports a black screen for ambience—
no heat required on our hot summer weekend.
Antique rugs thrill my eyes and delight my bare feet.
A cozy and sweet bathroom suite
marvelously has all you need.
Our comfy escape is lit by thoughtful lamps—
new and old—just right.
The warm sensation of Casa Magdalena
and the memory of its twig encircled lamp
follow me home.

My Favorite Things

God's grace and favor
Sunshine and rain
A warm soft breeze
Birds chirping, crickets cricking
Windmills and wind sculptures
Trees and swings
Children playing

Family and friends
Shopping and sharing
Cherished memories, happy tears
Genuine smiles, friendly hugs
Gut-wrenching, tear-jerking laughter
Kindness and sharing
The rhythm of downhome blues

Long peaceful walks—
        in the sand
        in the city
        off the beaten path
Golden sunsets, ocean waves
Tropical island mist
Tradewinds and fiery torches

Celebrations, happy endings
Fireworks

Poetry and all things beautiful
Prayers sent and prayers received
A good night's sleep
Reading and music

Road trips, travel
A glass of wine, a Moscow mule
Shellfish and catfish
Flowers and mountains

Candle-lit romantic dinners
Sweet aromas, good company
Another's touch
Simple thoughtful pleasures
Rainbows and waterfalls
Tomorrow's promise

18K: Refined Golden Sentiments

Born Day Thoughts 2021

I left the warmth of my mother's womb
to enter the world with all its gloom
I fully rely on a higher being
to direct my life's divine meaning.

My inner strength comes from above
I freely share tremendous love
Thank you, Lord, for my special day
I have all I need…You paved the way.

I do not worry, nor do I fear
Your protective shield is always near
You and I have much to say
Your glorious words are all I pray.

I'm cautious in my private thoughts
No altered facts, truth can't be bought
I want all to see Your light in me
To sense my heartfelt empathy.

I'll honor you in everything I do
I excitedly start this year anew
I'll strive to give the world my best
Please, Father, say I passed the test!

Empty Space

Be not deceived by an empty space
Engage all your senses
Feel the invisible essence of what
occupied what appears to be vacant
With every breath, take in what
you cannot see—matter and energy
from what came before Life—
eternal and infinite—
goes on and on and on
With each breath, imagine what will follow.

I inhale and receive the love that
God pours into me…
I keep all that I need
My soul is changed
I add my essence and send the remainder
out into the world
Love occupies that space…
It is not empty!

Hand in Hand

Rise up higher with every step
Don't look back for things you left
Beyond closed doors opportunity waits
Step boldly into your future's fate

Take my hand and trust my lead
As I share wisdom, please take heed
I'll take you places where I have been
To richly engage your mind within

Throughout my life I've seen a lot
A few of the lessons, I forgot
The critical ones are vivid and clear
Experience helped me face my fears

Our linked hands are a solid bond
If you need me, I'll gladly respond
I wish you joy, adventure, and growth
The rewards ahead will bless us both

Extend your free hand to someone else
Do not keep wisdom to yourself
Reach out to others as you rise
Share the things that made you wise.

Steppingstones

I pay homage to those who paved my way
with steppingstones of wisdom and grace.
I follow the light that guides my feet,
step by step to their appointed place.

Not every stone was stable.
Not every stone is firmly set.
Yet every stone advances me
one step closer to the next.

When unstable, God takes my hand.
If my footing slips, He carries me.
Assuredly I continue my journey
in bold pursuit of my life's destiny.

I stand on the shoulders of giants—
first my parents, then my big brother,
plus, gallant leaders Bill Pitts, Dan Raybon,
and the Nilons, among others.

I'm one of many whose path you set
with hopeful expectations
Your selfless impact made a difference
throughout the world and nation.

Someday I'll take my final step,
leaving my last footprint on earth.
It will conclude my life's guided path,
traveled since the day of my birth.

I will leave behind my loving essence.
I will have shared many inspiring words.
My literary footprint shall live forever
as minds across the globe are stirred.

Triumphantly I will move into heaven
reuniting with loved ones I've known.
I will thank all my heroes for setting
the steppingstones that led me home.

Abecedarian Wisdom

Affirm your beliefs and pray for a
Better world of good intentions
Consciously care about mother earth…let us
Do good deeds…make room for
Every person without fear of scarcity
Free our hearts of hatred, our minds of
Greed…accept that all people
Have merit…our words and actions are
Instrumental to humanity's resurgence…
Joyfully extend your true self—be
Kind…be generous
Love intently, knowing what really
Matters…suspend judgment
No one exists above the other…how
Often will you reach out—or reach back
Prepare for and expect success…
Query your thoughts for ways to show
Respect…always, demand respect
Settle for nothing less
Trust cautiously and responsibly…seek
Understanding when tensions rise
Very soon you will appreciate
Why these things are crucial…a
Xeric-like mind
Yearns for empathy, the only path to our
Zealous collective quest for love!

Let's Sing for the Unsung

Who sings for the unsung,
the quiet heroes among us?
Silent—not because they
have no lyrics or cannot speak…
Rather, because they are ignored repeatedly—
their voices dismissed.
They have plenty to say, amazing stories to tell.

It's time we listened to their cries:
       their soprano shrills
       their alto moans
       their protests of tenor
       their baritone notes of despair
Listen to their hopeful songs of hopelessness
       hummed because the world does not hear
       hummed because no one seems to care.

We must all sing for the unsung
Silence is not an option!
I can't retreat until we share their truth—our truth!
Let's sing for:
       the hungry child
       the frightened teen
       the struggling parents
       the silenced victim
       the roofless man, woman, child
       the closeted gay
       the undocumented worker
       the trafficked nanny
       the depressed
       the sick and shut-in
       the powerless people throughout the world!

Let's tell their stories and lift them up
Together, we can change their songs
Together, we can improve their outlook
Together, let us sing a song of boundless hope!

More Alike than Different

Singer Chaka Khan said it best,
"I'm every woman…"
And that includes Jane Austen!
It does not matter that I am Black
Nor does the color her skin lacked
Hearts echo a cadence of blended beats
All bodies require water and food to eat
Rest eases our minds, renews our strength
My day and your day are the same length
All nights conclude with a brand-new day
We greet joy and pain in the same way
Your body, my body—God's creations
We dream with hopeful expectations
I want to know you and you to know me
Loving our likeness fosters empathy.

My Tree

To the tree, a gift, planted in my name
       May your roots bind deeply in fertile earth
       May you cling to the river to quench your thirst
       May you be firmly anchored and nourished
       May you thrive as you are pruned by nature
       May you avert the ravages of climate change
       May you avoid perilous winds and drought
       May raging fires keep their distance
       May lightning never seek or find you
       May hostile insects not pursue you
       May you absorb the sun's nourishing rays
       May you flourish in the refreshing rain
       May the seasons be gentle and kind to you
       May you shelter God's creatures, big and small
       May birds dwell and sing on your limbs
       May you provide shade from the sun's hot rays
       May your colors delight in every season
If you are an evergreen, may you be forever green

My gift, my tree, may you know my prayer:
Live long and mighty until God says it's time.

Loving Outdoors

My soul rejoices in the glorious outdoors
I'm lured by the smell of fresh-cut grass
Playful critters adorn the fence
Alluring butterflies dance through the air
The doves sing a sweet serenade
I am merrily stirred and calmed at once.

Billowing clouds release tantalizing raindrops
Roaring whispers of invisible wind
sway through the trees
The gentle breeze flirts with my spirit
as I delight in the windchime's musical range.

I savor the gift of open space wonders—
the seen and especially, the unseen.
Blackbirds move twigs from bush to tree
They build bassinets in the evergreens—
homes for their young, my future choir.
When the sun returns after the rain
I excitedly search for rainbows…
I am *Joy*. I am *Peace*. I am *Happy*!

Joy in My Swing

Your love appears in the form of a swing
My heart's desire—your intention to bring
Joy into my life, the calm I needed
To erase stress, my dear, you succeeded
I swing back and forth, immersed in the trees
Evergreen columns, you planted with ease
You sculpt them yearly with deliberate care
Side by side, like us—a perfect pair
Beyond the trees, God's bounty appears
Birds and windchimes, sweet sounds I hear
The grass is greener on our coveted side
Our provisions of nature reach far and wide
Faraway mountains, cottonwoods, and brush
At home in my swing, I slow my mind's rush
My swing brings peace and total awe
The joy I feel is tender and raw
This serene space is my personal retreat
My muse dances to my heart's happy beat
The endless sky offers clouds galore
Majesty encircles me—so much to adore
I smile at the squirrels, bunnies, and flowers
Before you know it, I've been swinging for hours!

Spinning

I am captivated by the glorious spin
of teal and copper metal,
controlled by the wind.
I surrender—often—to
the enticing sculpture
outside my window.
With centered stillness,
I am transported by vivid visions of others.

I gleefully gaze at windmills
looming over the plains, long ago and now.
They stop me in my tracks,
commanding a photo—
as if I won't remember.
I am entranced by their submission
to the laws of nature.

Spinning wheels hypnotize and mesmerize.
I am utterly enthralled by the paced
revolution of the massive wind turbine.
Why am I so charmed, I wonder.
Is it their rotation,
or their mindless conformity?
Perhaps I'm reminded of the circle of life—
its divine cycle and orbit—
and I am enchanted by that!

Stand Taller

Young students show up thirsty like sponges
eager and ideally primed to learn.
Educators must discern
how best to water those sponges.
Teachers hold the world in their hands.
Our future awaits the outcome of their work.
Our world depends on the education poured
into every sponge—the student.
Warmly receive and fill them with knowledge
Challenge them
Support them
Spark their curiosity
Satisfy their thirst with mentoring
so they may fully absorb insight and vision.
Hydrate their minds and encourage them
       to stand on the foundation of goodness
       to stand for something greater than themselves
       to stand firm in their beliefs
       to stand up for themselves and others.
Let's stand with students as pillars of wisdom
Let's be their anchors
Let's boost their belief that they are
tomorrow's great promise
Let's watch them rise up and stand taller.

Look at the Poets

I marvel at the vessels of grace—
like-minded creative messengers.
If the world seeks a model of love
and understanding,
just look at the poets!
We live around the world
We live in your homes
We live in your communities
We work with you
We fellowship with you
We complete your friendship circles
We are everywhere.

Watch us transcend boundaries and barriers.
Our connections are colorless.
Our impact is colorful.
We are one—
one in purpose
one in community
one in determination
to make a difference.
The time for poetry is now—
Always has been
Always will be
Look at the poets!

22K: Bright Golden Luminaries

Colorful Photo

I adore a black and white photo
lavish with color…
What color is love
What color is family
What color is happy
In this cherished image, all are black and white.

Her dress and coat
adorn her divinely carved body—
the body that bore legacies of their endless love.
Bliss travels through her smiley eyes
gazing upward, loving
and dreamy, fixed on him.
He knows it…the tilt of his hat shows it!
You tall, dark, and handsome man—my daddy—
the talk of the town.
I wish I'd been old enough to remember you
in that suit, worn like a badge of honor.
Tirelessly you labored for our family of eight.
So did she—my mother
who passionately catered to your every desire.
You both deserved a good time on the night
of your colorful black and white photo.
I hope it was passionate.
I hope it was grand!

Reflection

I am the whole spectrum—
a refined vessel of light—
a colorful reflection of everything good.
I am utterly pleased
with who I am.
My skin is a combination
of my daddy's Louisiana chocolate
and my mother's Mississippi red.
Call me Caramel Frappuccino,
no whip.
My hips are
fittingly curved
like a country road
winding along the river.
My breasts—though not
majestic—are
suitable foothills.
I'm good with that!
My butt is not
apple-bottom round
but what does that matter.
It is not about my body!
It's about my essence.
Respect what's inside my head—
well-read—
bursting with kind thoughts
and full of dreams.
Faithfully loyal,
I am a rich gumbo
of love and poetry,
a rue with the perfect hue—
ready to be served…hot.
I'm ready to touch the world!

Double Blessings

To our beloved double blessings,
my amazing granddaughters,
always remember that you are our gift…
Our miraculous, precious, and glorious gift.
You, Kyla and Kyli, were meant to be!
I joyfully remember God's whisper
His voice, resolute, and clear
His generous promise to me,
as my plane ascended
above the clouds over Georgia,
over eleven years ago.
"You will have two babies,"
God said,
despite what the doctors said.
And I believed Him with all my heart…
with every sense of my being.

Then against all odds
on a lovely Monday afternoon,
you both arrived fighting,
as if your lives depended on it…
as if your mommy's life depended on it!
Kyla Rock and Kyli Roll,
that's what your uncle called you.
You were fragile yet strong—
barely visible beneath the gear
that fought with you and for you.

Your presence…divinely striking.
You inhabited our prayers.
And today, you are our answered prayers.
You are fierce,
you are gifted, kind, and humble.
You are destined for greatness.
Above all, you are God's promise—
Boldly and beautifully fulfilled!

TO SOAR WITH THE GREATS,
WE HAVE TO DO GREAT THINGS GREATLY.
~ Zaneta Varnado Johns ~

The Man You See
A Tribute to Darryl at Retirement

The man you see
was once a child with promise
Like all children he deserved a shot
The man you see is my brother
Six of us sprouted from the same branch
of a tree deep-rooted in love
Money was fairly lacking
though the man you see
never lacked confidence or love.

He traveled an extraordinary journey
from Hammond, Louisiana's
Mooney Avenue, to our nation's capital
The man you see picked strawberries
His school year began late
to reduce exposure to unbearable heat
The man you see is never late
nor does he shy away from heat
He mowed lawns—or better said
he cut grass before the days
of power mowers and water bottles
Nearly dehydrated on a sweltering afternoon
one homeowner gave him a discarded can
for garden hose water…Imagine that!

The man you see was an athlete
Determined and focused
he understood the nexus
between effort and execution
He was advised by his high school counselor
to forego college
Always the navigator of his own ship
he boldly dismissed her counsel—
seeing it for what it was.

The man you see was intentionally plucked
like a ripe strawberry
from his dispiriting surroundings
His mentor reached back
for that promising young Black man
and paved his road to Colorado
The man you see is a buffalo
with a heart of CU black and gold
His life was transformed
by education, exposure, and hard work.

No stranger to heartache
the man you see embraced
the advice of our father
to not only achieve greatness—but to be great
As he ascended
he left standing room on his shoulders
He reached back and rendered a steady current
to lift the wings of so many others
He was once told that you can't save everybody…
Yet I have watched him try, time and again
as he relentlessly saved
everybody he could!

The man you see is deliberate
His every move was determined
by the one he made before
He grows wherever he is planted
When life's trials found him
He found courage
With agony as his balm
the man you see clung to his branch
and always found triumph.

The man you see loves people
Neither status nor position
can overshadow his pride in
maneuvering an eighteen-wheeler
or his love of down-home blues
The man you see sheds his suits
rolls up his sleeves
He eats Louisiana gumbo and seafood
outdoors while swatting mosquitoes
with a smile on his face—with no complaints.

The man you see harbors no bitterness
Remember that can of water
on that hot summer day?
Never to thirst again
the man you see secured a future
where he drinks from his own well
Were that woman to visit him now
he would undoubtedly offer her
some homemade strawberry wine
served in a custom-designed
Poetic Forecast wine glass!

The man you see is a family man
First a son, a brother, an uncle
Later a spouse, prideful father, and grandfather
He wears these hats like a badge of honor
The man you see takes no wooden nickels
Moreover, he is known to turn
nickels and dimes and quarters
into airline tickets for his mother
or to evoke million-dollar smiles
on the faces of young children.

Darryl Wayne Varnado is the man you see
executive vice president—soon to be retiree
In the words of one of the greatest men I know,
Smiles to you, my dear brother!

"There's a poem in that."
Lisa Tomey

She Is…

She is poetry—pulsing and prolific
She is a beacon of light
She is a nexus for poetic voices
She is a partner, mother, and friend
She is a devoted spiritual warrior
She is a woman who makes a difference
She is a phenomenal gift to humanity.

She is thunderous—lush with creativity
She is generous—with a desire to inspire
She is tenacious—an advocate of kindness
She is wondrous—a delightful modern artist
She is curious—an avid seeker of new voices
She is rigorous—in her pursuit of knowledge
She is fabulous—a living embodiment of love
She is amorous—passionate in her expressions
She is vociferous—on the page or virtual stage
She is pervious—accessible and accommodating
She is prosperous—a champion who advances others
She is meticulous—a promising innovative publisher.

We have no history…what we have is now.
She is Lisa, last name, Tomey
She is…my prized poetic sister!

Tribute to Amanda Gorman

Amanda Gorman is poetry in motion
She is a supreme vessel
of divine words—
an intentional courier
sent by God.
A perfectly packaged gift,
she is not too this,
not too that.
Poised, petite, pretty, prepared!
Moreover, she honorably delivers:
        always ready to step up,
        always ready to touch our souls.

A single mother's legacy,
singularly, she inspires
all generations among us
and all generations that follow.
She empowers children
who struggle with speech—
        who can't say "tomorrow,"
        who pause when saying,
        "right" or "wrong."
The boys and girls who
nervously approach their "Rs,"
like my granddaughter,
are now empowered
        now encouraged
        now accepted
because of Amanda Gorman's
fine brave example.

Whether reciting with silence
or reciting with music
Whether accompanied by
graphics or dance,
Amanda Gorman is fluid like water.
She surrounds her listener
with every sense of her being.
Phenomenal is not sufficient
to capture her essence…
This poetic comet
soared across millions of miles
wearing a crown of greatness!

She travels as one with her words,
from formation to target,
in pulsating harmony
like an instrument and its parts.
Her expression, like keys
of her own piano—
like strings of her own harp.
She shared thunderous truths
with eloquent singsong solutions
of grace, healing, and hope.

In her five-minute
momentous recital
Amanda Gorman elevated poetry
to its proper altitude.
We now hunger for her words
like loaves and fishes
meant to feed the masses—
meant to restore humankind.

Her profound words
attach themselves to you
and infiltrate your soul.
      You can't not listen
      You can't un-hear
Her voice, like a stalker,
won't leave…you don't want it to!
The choice is not yours
or mine
because grace showed up
in a perfectly packaged,
perfectly oiled,
unshakable godly messenger.
Her name is Amanda Gorman!

High Voltage: The Love of a Beautiful Lamp
In Honor of Cynthia Hightower-Jenkins

When a meteor streaks across the heavens
billions are summoned to watch—
as was the case with Cynthia Hightower-Jenkins!
Her light shone so brightly that God
called her home early
Early because her work was done
Early because her crown was waiting!

Cynthia's light illuminated others
Her brightness was so lavish
that God had to diffuse it with love!
When the sun and moon meet
one eclipses the other
When one and Cynthia met, the beam
was sure to be magnified in its brilliance.

How great it feels
to love someone I have not met
No platform could contain
Cynthia's magnetic spirit
The current of her electrifying presence
traveled purposefully—
directly into our hearts.
I know love when I see it!

This luminous lamp called
Cynthia Hightower-Jenkins
was not only all things beautiful…
Cynthia was light—inside and out!
She loved with intensity
Adored wife, mother, activist, fashion designer,
business leader, and so much more.

God has spoken—
Beautiful Cynthia, your crown is waiting!

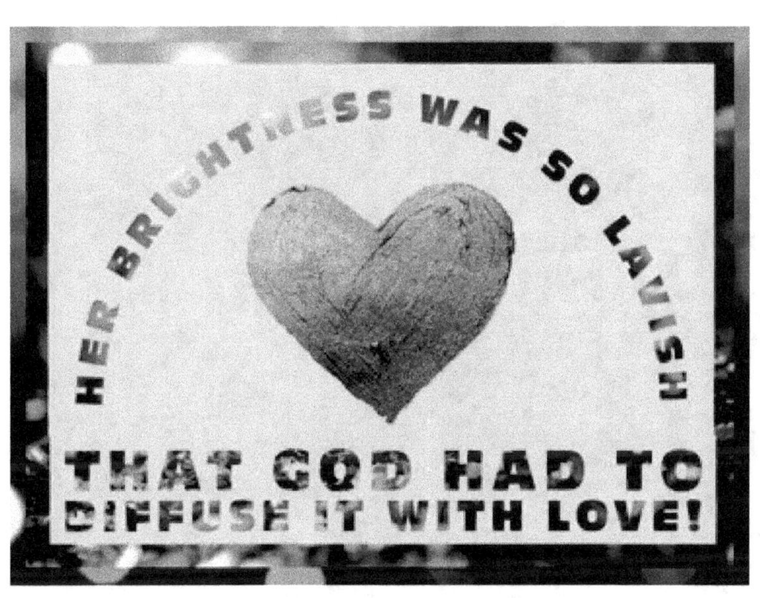

HER BRIGHTNESS WAS SO LAVISH
THAT GOD HAD TO
DIFFUSE IT WITH LOVE!

Ms. Maggie

Dear Ms. Maggie
Approaching 91!

Dear Ms. Maggie,
beloved mother of men—
six sons reared and raised
singlehandedly
by you…their rock
Emerson, Marshal, Donald
Earl, Pierre, and Silas
       six honorable men
       six reflections of you
       six men who honor
and dearly adore you
because you've shown
       love unfiltered
       strength unwavering
       spirit untethered
       courage unequalled
       actions unleashed
Your First Saturday gatherings,
a cozy circle of family
who savored your tasty food.
Those events, never unattended
as you commanded
R.E.S.P.E.C.T.
You, the unforgettable Ms. Maggie!

Dear Ms. Maggie,
Our lives are intertwined
Never a meeting face to face
But we have met!
Decades ago, by example
You set in motion a stern message
from which I benefit.
Your bold pursuit of dreams
were halted by no one.
Dreams fulfilled and shared
with Janet—my sister.
Your solid example
resonates to this day…
Passed on to me
through Janet—twin to my husband
Encourager to my dreams
Dreams fulfilled and shared
Just like yours.

Dear Ms. Maggie,
Rejoice as you wake each morning
awaiting the sun
to shine through your window
to wake you once again!
Approaching ninety-one, still vibrant
        still thankful
        still wanting
not just to be alive
but to be LIVING!
Ms. Maggie, you are indeed LIVING.

You're still in charge
still commanding the respect
you so rightfully deserve.

You create treasures
to honor all women,
courageous women like you—
who came before us.
You create treasures
to bless all the women
who follow…
In the month to honor women
your elegant creations
mirror your light and love.

Women adorned with objects
saved from your vast journeys
        from Colorado to Turkey
        from Turkey to Colorado
        from Colorado to California
        and so many places in between.
Your cherished art surrounds you
like sunshine and family,
comforting reminders
of a life well lived.
Dear Ms. Maggie, keep on LIVING!

Tribute to the Africa Agenda
Inspired by Founder George Bamu

I salute Africa Agenda's noteworthy cause.
Your demand for truth gives journalists pause.
It is no simple task—your honorable quest
Your tireless effort gives the world your best.
I searched the definition of truth online
What I discovered truly boggled my mind.
Is fact considered truth, or is truth a fact?
The more I searched, the more clarity I lacked!
Reality and perception are rival constructs.
Your pursuit of truth, these rivals disrupt.
One man's truth is another man's lie.
But Africa's resilience cannot be denied.
Disproportionate focus on the continent's ills
ignores decades of progress and Africa's goodwill.
You confront unfair words or tones unbefitting.
Reporters should take note that you are never quitting.
They should recycle plastic and not Africa's news.
Profit motivated coverage is a shameful abuse!
Your agenda upholds Africa's bold reputation.
Integrity is expected from all reporting nations.
What's sincere is your noble purpose and spirit.
What matters is Africa's truth—the world must hear it!

Tribute to Jason Merriweather
Commissioned by Pastor Bruce Lee Merriweather

When God called, Jason triumphantly answered.
It was the most important call of his life.
God said, "No more pain or strife, Dear Son,
Your selfless work on earth is done."

This July baby became a loving family man.
Providing for his family was Jason's daily plan.
With a great sense of humor, Jason laughed a lot.
Party after party, he was the favored mascot.

Jason loved antique cars, especially that '56 Chevy.
Tended with a strong foundation, his anchors were heavy.
Intentionally named Jason LaRon, not Jason Lee…
That fifth-generation middle name was not meant to be.

Dad Bruce Lee Merriweather boldly broke that chain.
The name Jason means healing, chosen not in vain.
Jason was a golden chip off the old block
He was influenced by elders who showed him a lot.

Spiritual leadership was sometimes considered.
Service to his community is what Jason delivered.
He was employed by Kaiser; on occasion, he cooked.
His passion for baseball cannot be overlooked.

Jason was a father of four lovely girls—
Q'Aura, Niyah, Mia, and Leilah—the center of his world.
Beloved husband, son, brother, colleague, and friend—
When Jason smiled at you, you felt his love within.

Jason LaRon Merriweather was loved beyond measure.
We thank God for the memories he left us to treasure!

We Are They

This is our season
our summer in the midst of winter
where we shed our coats, our boots
We leave behind the joyful chaos
of family and friends
We shed the stress
of everyday life
We steal away to our happy place
of paradise
We arouse years of memories
our minds free, schedule clear
ready to create this season's story.

Do you remember that couple—
the elders we admired in '97?
We are they!
From the restaurant's lanai
we watched as they walked
hand in hand
Their stride as one
moving in blissful unison
down that tourist filled
sidewalk in Kona
Perhaps returning from dinner
or strolling for exercise
I imagined they were residents
fortunate to live there
In that moment
I claimed that sidewalk for us.

Twenty-four years later
we are that charming couple
walking hand in hand
claiming sidewalks wherever we go
We long for that sidewalk today
in Kona or Kihei, Kapaa or Princeville
We long for days without structure
no boundaries or stress
Only joy with time devoted only
to us, that elderly couple in Kona
Occasionally we part
only to enhance
our savored time together.

Hours and hours of favored music
songs repeated and songs anew
Our wondrous day rides
enthralled with island splendor
Our bewitching nights
enthralled in glory—ours
Sunrise awaits with roosters crowing
tropical birds serenade our walks
fragrant flowers, brides, and grooms
lava flows and tropical mist
We're seduced by the ocean
enticed by waterfalls
intrigued by rainbows
mesmerized by sunsets
radiant and golden, just like us.

What we need this year
is imagination
to encounter the pleasures
of that sidewalk in Kona
Here we are
Better…wiser…cautious
held captive by winter
with willful summer mindsets
Still laughing
Still loving
Still holding hands
Still hearing that music
Still seeking rainbows
Still enjoying our sunsets
Still together
Because you loved me
in stereo
with both your heart and mind!

We're seduced by the ocean
enticed by waterfalls
intrigued by rainbows
mesmerized by sunsets
radiant and golden, just like us.

24K: Pure Solid Gold

One Day

One day, homes will be filled with people
      not homeless anymore.
One day, clean water will flow freely from the earth's core.
One day, opportunities for all children
      will follow God's plan.
One day, inequality disappears as justice reigns
      over the land.
One day, the air is clear because we cared
      for Mother Earth.
One day, food is plentiful because we'll reward
      the farmers' worth.
One day, teachers are heralded as sculptors of tomorrow.
One day, students have all they need without
      a need to borrow.
One day, hatred is replaced by love which overflows.
One day, greed is erased while love steadily grows.
One day, we'll have no wars, fighting no longer exists.
One day, across the globe, only goodness will persist.
One day, our world returns to the garden that God created.
One day, peace results from knowing we are all related.
One day, we'll welcome families no matter how they look.
One day, patience will rule despite how long it took.
One day, respect becomes a nonnegotiable trait.
One day, humanity is restored before it is too late.
Let's make *one day* today!

Covered by Prayer

When darkness looms, I retreat within my soul.
I am brave because I know what covers me—
I'm covered by the prayers of my ancestors
Prayers from Africa's Republic of Cameroon
Prayers from the bottom of the ships—
vessels that drowned dreams and freedom
in the deepest darkest depths of the ocean.
I'm covered by their incessant prayers for survival
and their woeful prayers for home.
I am covered by the prayers of strong tortured men—
the men who landed in darkness—tormented
Prayers that cleansed their soiled battered bodies
Prayers that replenished their broken spirits
Prayers that relinquished their royalty
Prayers that preserved their regal essence
Prayers that calmed unspeakable anguish
Prayers that caused them to love despite peril
I follow the light of my resilient people
who prayed for me through centuries of hell
I'm covered by the prayers that brought us through
Prayers that buoyed us to rise above
Prayers that protect me when the outside looms dark.

No Footprints
Inspired by Shauna Seals

When life's squabbles fiercely erupt
When your burdens become unbearable
When your pain is too intense
When no words provide comfort
When the despair is overwhelming
When your light becomes dim
When your sunken eyes are swollen
When dark nights lead to darker days
When looking down feels better than up
When you are gently lifted and carried
When your way comes out of no way
When you can't recall progression
When troubled water no longer troubles you
When your season of trials ends
When your tears dry up
When you look down, perplexed
When you see footprints that are not your own
There is no need to look again
You know the answer—
You left no footprints because God carried you through.

Everyone Get Ready

Honoring Curtis Mayfield's "People Get Ready"

Everyone get ready
There's a movement formin'
The masses have spoken
Their message is clear
You have not listened
You've dismissed their stories
It's time we all wake up
to what matters now

Everyone get ready
The truth is upon us
There's no denying
all the pain you've caused
Our healing begins
with minds wide open
Take nothing for granted
We must act today

All people are equal
Do not fear my sisters
Seek understanding
Build connections now
Make room for all
no matter their color
We're in this together
We must save this world

So, everyone get ready
'cause the world is watchin'
Keepers of brothers
from across the globe
Love is the key
Let your hearts receive it
Regard for all people
will heal all mankind!

Whispers from Heaven

I welcome the whispers—softly spoken—
uttering, "I'm so proud of you!"
When love calls from heaven, I smile.
Angelic reassuring voices appear
just when I need a nudge.

Tender messages from my loved ones
comfort me in perpetuity on earth.
I receive and retain them
deep within my soul.
It is well with my soul.
Keep whispering—I'm listening.

No More Violence

Noble giants demonstrated long ago
how peace can bring about change
Gandhi, Mother Teresa, Martin Luther King Jr.
We must never forget their names.

Imagine if they were alive today
Would they feel their lives were in vain?
If they saw the reckless attachment to weapons,
I expect it would trigger deep pain.

So, let's make love our next pandemic
Allow love to virally infect our minds
Paint LOVE brightly on all the weapons
So that peace can restore humankind.

Place ourselves in our neighbors' shoes
Reject hatred and greed at all times.
If God's image appeared at the end of a scope,
surely, that will eliminate violent crimes.

Thanksgiving

Thank you, Lord, for the life you gave us
Thank you for the sacrifices made for us
Thank you for the shelter around us
Thank you for the heroes among us
Thank you for the joy between us
Thank you for the experience behind us
Thank you for the blessings before us
Thank you for the love surrounding us
Thank you for the power within us
Thank you for the foundation beneath us
Thank you for the sunshine above us
Thank you for the strength you provide us
Thank you for the grace you give us
Thank you for the wisdom you pour into us
Thank you for no weapon formed against us
Thank you for your continuous watch over us
Thank you for the generations that follow us
Thank you for the heavens awaiting us
Lord, I am grateful, and I thank you for everything!

My Last Prayer

When God calls me home,
I pray that my light is brightly shining.
When I reach for God's hand,
may the light surrounding me brighten
as my internal beam dims.

I pray that my life honors God's commands—
      that I used every gift intended to make a difference
      that every word I shared spread love
      that I was kind to others and myself
      that my "Well done" was rightfully deserved.

I pray that I am ready.
No more words are needed—none left unsaid.
I pray that I am weightless—
no burdens, no sorrows, no regrets.
I pray that only love is left behind—
that my family knows that I loved them dearly.
I pray they'll know that they made me proud—
so proud that all in heaven will hear about them.
I pray they'll know that while my body is no longer,
my soul lives within them.
I ask them to carry me as I carried
the souls of my own dearly departed.

To my friends, you gave me everything.
I will sing your praises too.
Relive our stories, our heartfelt laughter.
Hold fast to our endless love.

To everyone touched by my ink,
thank you for accepting what God had for you.
Use what you need and share the rest.

I pray that you are covered by infinite love,
protection, and divine favor.
Always remember that what matters is love.
I'm out!

About the Author

Zaneta Varnado Johns is a 2-time bestselling author who believes that every word shared is an opportunity to love. She published her debut book of poetry, **Poetic Forecast**: *Reflections on Life's Promises, Storms, and Triumphs*, in November 2020. Johns is a contributing author in the #1 international bestseller **Voices of the 21st Century**: Resilient Women Who Rise and Make a Difference (WSA Publishing, February 2021) and in **Voices of the 21st Century**: Conscious Caring Women Who Make a Difference (WSA Publishing, February 2022). Both **Voices of the 21st Century** books feature Johns' poems as the Dedication page.

Johns is a contributing author of poetry and prose in numerous anthologies and international literary journals. Since her debut, she has been highly sought after by the international poetry community for recitations and collaborations. Her poems have been recognized by Sargam for Literary Interactions and the Passion of Poetry. Her poem, *"New Wonderland,"* written with Pratibha Savani of the United Kingdom, was recognized by the Passion of Poetry as Best Collaborative Poem in October 2021.

An engaging poet, Johns is active online at open mic events, poetry recitations, and promotional interviews. She appeared internationally on WSA-TV, Sargam for Literary Interactions, Progressive Literary & Cultural Society, and India's *The Fertile Brains* poetry meet marking the International Day of Non-Violence. Johns was a featured poet on Defy Domestic Abuse's video in honor of Domestic Violence Awareness Month and appeared on *New York Parrot Literary Corner—EP199: Zaneta Varnado Johns and Her Inking Hub.*

Recently serving as the keynote speaker at the Africa Agenda Summit, Johns is not slowing down. In November 2021, she joined the Passion of Poetry Administrative team as a Moderator. This former human resource leader spent twenty-nine rewarding years at the University of Colorado where she was recognized as one of the *2007 Women Who Make a Difference.* Johns resides in Westminster, Colorado, USA.

Contributing Poets

Sarfraz Ahmed is the author of **Stab the Pomegranate**, **Eighty-Four Pins,** and a children's book, **My Teacher's an Alien!** with illustrator Natasha Adams. He is the co-author of **Two Hearts** with Annette Tarpley. He is globally active in open mics and live recitations. He was recognized as a World Contributor Poet in 2021 by Poetry and Literature World Vision for his contribution to poetry. His poems are featured in numerous anthologies. Sarfraz is a professional Careers Adviser and an administrator for the *Passion of Poetry* Facebook platform, founded by Annette Tarpley. His poetry books are available on Amazon. His children's book is available at Green Cat Books. He resides in the East Midlands-United Kingdom. Learn more about Sarfraz Ahmed on Facebook or Instagram.

Pratibha Savani is a UK Poet, Artist, and author of **Tangles + Knots**. Her debut book uniquely combines her art and writing with mindfulness and wellbeing themes. Published in *Open Door Poetry Magazine* and in several anthologies, Pratibha is inspired by the cosmos, nature, and spirituality. She is a creative soul that believes possibilities exist, and she likes to explore the boundaries by playing with words, layout and defying the rules with her inventive expressions on Instagram and Facebook as: *Pratibha Poetry Art.*

Gratitude

I extend sincere gratitude and respect to:

James J. Johns II and Kelli Rynae Jackson, my perpetual
pillars
Leslee Carpenter, for divine creative discussions
Women Speakers Association
Prolific Pulse Poetry
Garden of Neuro Institute
Passion of Poetry
Sargam for Literary Interactions
Black and Gold Project Foundation
New York Parrot Literary Corner
Progressive Literary & Cultural Society

If you can imagine the brilliance of the rarest diamond or the
stillness of the darkest night, you will know how much you
have warmed my heart. As the author of **After the Rainbow**:
Golden Poems, I am because of you. May you be keenly
blessed.

Jane
Austen
animal
fiends
POETIC
FORECAST
VOICES OF THE
21ST CENTURY
ZANETA V. JOHNS
Golden Books

Book Club Dialogue Prompts

To engage in deeper discussion, please consider these questions:

1. The author includes rainbows as one of her favorite things. How do you feel about rainbows?
2. Do you personally identify with any of the themes of the book or any specific poem? Which and why?
3. The use of gold designations for chapter titles is intriguing. How do you feel about the distinctions relative to the poetry collections found within each chapter?
4. The author enjoys celebrating people, including some she has not met. Which tribute stands out for you? Why?
5. If you were to pay tribute to someone, who would it be? Why?
6. The author was inspired early on by Nikki Giovanni and Maya Angelou. Discuss a specific poem that reminds you of either.
7. The poem, "Dear Ms. Maggie," was written to celebrate Ms. Maggie's 91st birthday. The author was inspired to learn that on November 7, 2021, Ms. Maggie spontaneously ran for ninety minutes on the sidewalk alongside the LA Marathon. Are you equally inspired? Discuss how physical activity relates to overall health and wellness.
8. What is your most golden takeaway from **After the Rainbow**?

Thank you for spending your time with this creation from my heart. Following is a poem from my previously published book, **Poetic Forecast**.

Golden Nugget: Poet's *Most Requested Poem*, from **Poetic Forecast**

What Matters

If your eyes met my eyes in the midst of a crisis,
Would their shape and color concern you?

If you felt my hands as they massaged your aching body,
Would you care about the pigmentation of my skin?

If I gave blood to replenish your low supply
Would you need to know that I looked like you?

If you were drowning and I dove in to assist you,
Would you reach toward me if you knew I was gay?

If you were hearing for the first time in your life,
Would you need for my voice to speak English only?

If your loved one lay sick and dying,
Would it matter to which god I prayed?

If I donated money to support your favorite cause,
Would you refuse it if you knew how I voted?

If the size of my heart increased each time I helped somebody,
Would you be more interested in the size of my body?

If you asked me to walk a mile in support of humanity,
Would you get impatient if I used my wheelchair?

If I said "no" and you assaulted me anyway,
Are you less guilty because I waited to report?

If my family seeks asylum in the USA,
Are we not welcome because our border is to your south?

If the police force keeps killing unarmed citizens,
Would you demand justice if they are African American?

With civil unrest during this global pandemic,
Trust me, we will soon realize what matters!

www.ingramcontent.com/pod-product-compliance
Lightning Source LLC
Chambersburg PA
CBHW070401200726
48294CB00003B/1031